Reading Gail Sher

Also by Gail Sher

Reading Gail Sher

Gail Sher

NIGHT CRANE PRESS

2016

ISBN: 978-0-9858843-9-0

072316

for Brendan

Contents

Preface

"Poems need prose precincts," Ted Hughes once wrote to a friend. Like animals, poems could become extinct if the poet didn't endow them with a "habitat." Critics and poets alike, he felt, have an obligation to *steward* the "achieved human voice" found in poetry.

"Achieved" is the important word. Writing-over-time accretes into a voice that rings of the poet and *that* grows her poems, gradually, into maturity.

This book is an attempt to locate and describe the "habitats" of my own poetry. In retrospect, and certainly not by design, it seems to have organized itself into phases:

1. *Radical Language Experiments, 1982-1997*

When I first began writing, everything was a test. I had no idea of writing "poetry." I never read poetry. I avidly read prose. But my *concerns*, as I reluctantly learned, were all of them of a poet, not a novelist, short story writer or essayist. I came to understand that I *am* a poet because I *think* like a poet. And it was singularly poets and poet-editors who first saw and supported my work.

An early distinguishing underlying feature—that my writing simply arose—remains to this day. I don't write what I already know, or perhaps, stated more exactly, since my writing stems primarily from the "linguistic unconscious"[1] and not from everyday consciousness, I find it a continual surprise.

2. *Asian-influenced work, 1997-2008*

Taking writing as a practice followed eleven years of studying Zen. Living a monastic life with its strict schedule of *zazen* (sitting meditation), assigned work, *dharma* talks, *dokusan* (interviews with one's teacher), and the concentrated reading of Zen texts immersed my mind and body in an ancient Japanese culture. Actually my Asian-influenced poetry derives, in addition to Japan, from India, China, and Tibet and draws from Zen *and* Tibetan Buddhism (both philosophy and practice) *and* Hinduism (both philosophy and practice) which I studied for many years after leaving the zendo.

---

[1] See *Poetry, Zen and the Linguistic Unconscious,* pp. 3-6.

In this aspect of my work, I re-imagined ancient Asian musical and literary forms using:

— *haiku* to create extended narratives[2]

— *haibun* (prose + *haiku*) to write biographies[3] and autobiography[4]

— four-lined Chinese *kanshi* to establish the rhythms of four book-length poems[5]

The foundation for *RAGA* was the Indian *raga* and for *DOHĀ* the Tibetan devotional song.

3. The Wisdom-Mind Collection, 2009-2013

Between 2009 and 2013 I wrote a series of books, beginning with *The Tethering of Mind to Its Five Permanent Qualities*, and culminating in *The Twelve Nidānas* and *Mingling the Threefold Sky* that are rooted in Tibetan Buddhist philosophy and

---

[2] *Five Haiku Narratives.*

[3] *The Haiku Masters: Four Poetic Diaries.*

[4] *The Moon of the Swaying Buds.*

[5] *Watching Slow Flowers; Once There Was Grass; redwind daylong daylong; Look at That Dog All Dressed Out in Plum Blossoms.*

dedicated to "stretching" English in order to create gaps so that Wisdom-Mind might flow through to the reader.[6] Wisdom and knowledge are different of course: the former cannot be grasped by the intellect alone. The idea in these poems is to not-quite-make-sense. The beauty (hopefully) of the surface language + the strategy of "approaching-narrative" first intrigues then *holds* a reader, allowing, in stillness, the dawning of a new kind of intelligence. As a poet I feel that this body of work is my most important.

4. Late Work, 2014-present

Sunny Day, Spring, Ezekiel, Pale Sky and *Elm* (in press) are examples of writing indirectly influenced by contemporary writers and twenty-five years of practicing psychotherapy. Compared to the earlier work they are more accessible yet, deeply interior, they too reside in a vacuum of silence.

---

[6] *Mother's Warm Breath, White Bird* and *The Bardo Books* were also written from this perspective.

*

The opening section of this book, "The *Way* of the Poem," details some of the linguistic strategies I've used to help a reader open to the inconceivable. Cumulatively they present the poem as a tool, poetry as a Path.

The next section, "The *Way* of the Living Word," is about the word itself—the body of the word, the mind of the word, the transmission that each word carries. Headings such as these alert the reader to a "take" on language that is visceral rather than cognitive. For reading my poetry, this is key.

The final section, "Late Work," addresses writing that speaks to a different part of the brain. Prose-like in appearance it makes room for the conceptual, yet remains rooted in the concerns that characterize my work as a whole.

Appendix I contains reviews by poets who have their own ideas about my work, and an early letter-to-the-editor I wrote prior to publishing my own poetry, defending a poet who whose work I felt was misunderstood but whose approach I admired and still do.

Appendix II contains chronologies of my external life circumstances and an internal, psychological history of my relationship with language.

Acknowledgments

The many people who have supported my writing
over the years are too numerous to recall. My
deepest apologies in advance to those precious
people whose help I remember but whose names
I can no longer remember. My heartfelt thanks to
them and to:

—Beau Beausoleil and Merry White Benezra who
saw, encouraged, wisely critiqued and supported my
work from its earliest beginnings.

—Robert Duncan, who attended my first poetry
reading at Beau Beausoleil's San Francisco bookstore.
He was standing in the back and after I read he called
out, "Would you read that again?" Afterwards, he
introduced himself and encouraged me to send what
I had read to a new poetry journal at the University
at Buffalo (SUNY), *Credences.* My work appeared
in the inaugural issue of that journal, along with
poetry by Duncan himself. It was my first poetry
publication.[7]

---

[7] "Nine Pieces," *Credences: A Journal of Twentieth Century
Poetry and Poetics,* New Series, vol. 1, no. 1, Buffalo: State
University of New York, 1981, pp. 16-20

—Robert Bertholf, editor of *Credences* and curator
of the Poetry Collection at the University at Buffalo,
who invited me to Buffalo to read, address his
graduate students and stay at his beautiful home
as a way of promoting my experiments in non-
conceptual poetic language.

—Keith and Rosmarie Waldrop who designed,
printed and published my early "retablo," *Broke Aide,*
in their elegant Burning Deck series, chose it as
an NEA selection for the Frankfurt Book Fair, and
remained supportive and available for many years.

—Charles Bernstein who attended every Village
reading I gave, and offered the kind of critical
affirmation that helps poets grow.

—Kathleen Fraser, whose perceptive analysis of my
first book, *From another point of view the woman
seems to be resting,* placed my work in an historic
line of modernist women poets—Gertrude Stein,
H.D., Lorine Niedecker—thereby recognizing in
today's women poets what the psychoanalyst Heinz
Kohut saw in modernist playwrights and composers:
the articulation of a hidden suffering characteristic of

our age, thus creating the possibility of new forms of wholeness.[8]

—Joey Simas who published *Rouge to beak having me* in his Paris-based Moving Letters Press in the days when poet-friend publishers were not rare, and translated a long section from *Broke Aide* into French for a French anthology of New American poets[9], something I didn't think was possible.

—Andrew Feenberg whose invitation to lecture to a group of innovative thinkers in business, the military and the sciences inspired the talk that lead to *Poetry, Zen and the Linguistic Unconscious.*

—Jessica Grim, co-founder, with Melanie Neilson, of *Big Allis*, the poetry journal that promoted the experimental work of women writers early in their careers—exactly my situation when they welcomed me into their first issue.

---

[8] Kathleen Fraser, "Overheard," *Poetics Journal*, no. 4, May 1984, pp. 98-105. On Kohut, see Gail Sher, *Poetry, Zen and the Linguistic Unconscious,* pp. 10-12.

[9] *49+1: Nouveaux Poètes Américains,* choisis par Emmanuel Hocquard et Claude Royet-Journoud. Royaumont (France), 1991, pp. 222-223.

—Leslie Scalapino, fellow former graduate student in English at UC Berkeley, who arranged for me to move into the apartment next to hers, and joined me for long walks around Berkeley and fun out-of-town trips to visit other poets. She read my work and offered invaluable criticism regularly and generously.

—Andrew Schelling, friend, poet, teacher, who attended my readings, shared the pleasures of co-writing Japanese style *renga* together, and honored me with reviews and jacket cover statements erudite beyond my dreams.

—Philip Whalen, fellow poet and fellow student at the San Francisco Zen Center, who took serious interest in my work and who, when he was living in Sante Fe with Baker-roshi, attended the reading that Leslie Scalapino and I gave in Albuquerque.

—Ben Friedlander, Pat Reed, David Sheidlower and Jessica Grim who were part of a poetry "neighborhood" that surrounded me and accompanied me through all the years of my poetic tests.

—Michael Basinski, Curator of the Poetry Collection

at the University at Buffalo, who has supported my work for over thirty years. Most recently, he and his knowledgeable staff, especially James Maynard, a Robert Duncan scholar, have been expertly archiving my books, manuscripts, correspondence, art, and all the paraphernalia related to the poetic struggle that has been uniquely mine.

To all of them I offer a deep bow of gratitude.

Introduction

"Language is beautiful even without us. Once it was put into motion it was beautiful."

— Beau Beausoleil

Before the Poem is the Poem

Because of the poem, the poem can happen.

Literature *does* work by "penetrating consciousness at a level not reached by the speech of everyday transactions." (Ted Hughes)

The poem, superseding event, is like a brain clicking away, thinking in riffs and patches and incomplete discrete phrases.

Yet the whole is intentional and feels authentic *because* it attends to the whispered voices in the gaps.

"Not often have I come upon words with so much mystery which at the same time seem so responsible. They have teeth" (a critic of my work).

This is the poet's gentleness.

And the dignity in her lines.

Its language, connected to itself by a kind of prayer, propels a search wherein nothing provable is unearthed, yet the act of opening one's mind creates a free moment in which existence itself speaks lucidly and candidly if not, strictly speaking, rationally.

And this is how the truth is grasped: feelingly.

The Double Life of A Poem

So there's the poem that let's you "in" (if you allow it to open you) but "in" is not the poem. "In" is your heart and mind.

Yet you read with your mind also.

Your mind reads the poem, which is your mind.

The poem itself disappears.

It is the you-before-the-you that is trying to read itself.

As long as you think this, there is dualistic mind.

But that same mind, entering the poem . . .

> She tries to feel her floor, but she is thinking about a cavity, something fluid like a worm and she wants to *say* the worm.
>
> A moan is a moan and where can it reside if not on her floor, the speech body of that word.
>
> She jerks it up but trips so that *she* is the

floor and the glue and the shame. *I have a habit of glue*, she confesses.

A flame of everything sears into shape, which is not the word, but the colorless basis of its Pure Land.[10]

---

[10] *Mingling the Threefold Sky*, p. 5.

The *Way* of the Poem

When a poem of uncertain portent maintains its own isolation and integrity, like music, an independent language all its own will sing the place, inviting the reader.

For music can perhaps be thought of as pure-logic divested of the bothersome friction of words.

Along with the words we ingest the pure logic that is realized on its own, with its own wit, its own far-infrared dialectic.

A handful of parentheses sets a mood for the optional and *that's* all you have, like the flick of a conductor's wand.[11]

> *geshé geshé*
> you hook the word
>
> o Usnisavijaya
> (Shukden of despoil)

---

[11] Parentheses don't contain. They *shield.* As Kathleen Fraser points out, they are also "a usuage which women continue to find useful in breaking out of a misleading sense of stability." *Poetics Journal*, no. 4, May 1984, p. 100.

to gull the sky
sweet gull of northwest flowers

I am tall
I am slow full
walker[12]

---

[12] *Who, a* Licchavi, p. 43.

Memory

A poem has its own memory.

And the poem's memory provides a *feeling* context to the private memory of each word.

Their inter-change creates a field.

"I SEE it," says a reader who then sallies along smelling all the flowers.

First seeing, then entering the poem's field, in part authors the poem's memory.

Actually poetry *is* memory, endowing words with a kind of eternity.

Allure

While the poet's oral rendering of her poem is a
powerful venue for the poem, sometimes *on the page*
a voice can be more "catchable."

Being drawn into its world, partaking of that world
such that for the moment of the poem, *you* are the
person, affected.

Certain poems, like Paris, so completely BELIEVE
in themselves that their world—even one word—
becomes an entire creed.

> I see a photograph of her throat, which is
> not the actual throat. *Where is her throat in
> the wake of <u>that</u>?* (I'm guessing *that* means
> *after* her throat.)[13]

---

[13] *White Bird*, p. 68.

Frisson

The frisson of a word rouses a reader.

As does the frisson of a phrase (the electrical atmosphere in its magnetic field).

The frisson of a word, the frisson of a phrase *is* the poem's event.

> I see the fish who is my brother. Its time is
> pink like mine. We flow in the same yard.[14]

When reading Gail Sher, stay with *that.*

----

[14] *The Bardo Books*, p. 3.

Tension-Sense Dialogue

A word does not designate.

A word speaks (jells) within its individual context and resting in the detail of its universal specificity is never just, say, "duck," or "Buddha" or "tit."

Add the presence of another word and "things" happen—a word gets tense.

Some things make words more tense, like following "thought" with "of" or taking a noun in the singular.

And sense (in our usual understanding)—sense dissipates tension.

Actually sense works for language in much the same way as background music for script.

The action rolls along but then someone says something off or there'll be a pause and if the background music captures everyone's secondary attention, no one even notices.

Without it (if we don't use sense in this way), all of the other aspects of a word are exposed and can work directly.

Non-sense

Sense, like a cart rambling down a long, linear road, carries a phrase not carried by all of the other aspects.

Scrambling-what-*would-be*-consecutive forces a mind to stop.

To space out *literally*.

"Let's *really* space out, not just haze but blast outside our ordinary sphere," the not-quite-sensical words urge.

It's unconscious, therefore powerful, increasing our chances of pausing ordinary mind's chatter.

> A body dissolves and there is no memory of its having been undissolving.

> Like a bird whose hair got swallowed of its color. It is sizeless, jigsawing red, as if red is the surrogate of all possible places.

> A man taps a bird on the window of its head. *He can dissolve with passing away,* someone says.

Then I am in my body but not captive in my body, because the reflection of my body as a "high" black bird got swallowed up.[15]

---
[15] *The Bardo Books*, p. 28.

Repetition

From here, one adds the element of repetition. (I almost said "passion.")

When a word repeats it seems more genuinely to be one's feeling.

Repetition soothes and instills desire. "Tell me again," "read it again," like a record one will play over and over and over, digging the groove inside the soul that played it over and over even before it was born.

Counting, a "take-off"—da-t'-da, da-t'-da, da-t'-da, da-t'-da—it's in the human gene.

The "hook" of the word creates the safety-of-environment. We need to feel safe to risk slipping through a gap.

Poetry *is* dangerous, after all.

Gaps

The marrow of the style is gaps. Hiatus and lucid gaps.

Lurking behind would be a story verging on revealing itself were the gaps colored in.

The reader gets an invite—"Please, dear reader, color me in"—such that the poem is co-creative, the revelation is co-creative, shaping itself to each individual's paradigm.

> Mother's warm breath, like a *plate* of breath. Yet it is old breath, having eaten many crackers.
>
> *My breath is a wall*, she whispers from *real* breath, instantly present to birds.
>
> The energy of the animal appears to be experienced internally, its breath (a shadow) withheld in its own stem.
>
> What's left of mind as a squirrel leaps out?[16]

----

[16] *Mother's Warm Breath*, p. 79.

Pacing a poem by breaths not only creates an intensity but also a sense of ongoingness.

For what is language and what is breathing, the one propelling and originating the other?

The words elude while the breaths make a philosophy.

Syntax *is* the motion.

Each word has it own syntax,

Searching Energy

Each word has a location so that when we hear a word, unconsciously we expect for it.

Just naturally, by virtue of the human mind.

We complete what is happening by *listening* it. (We HEAR the word into LIFE.)

The mind, activated by a word, allows its affective nature to touch it.

> Sparrows seem used, uninvented.

> Scaly mud, dull sky, colorless birds, remind me of my mind.

> To see the autumn leaves scatter in my home. (The longing they arouse as they lie on the wood turning red.)

> Is it of my body that they partake?[17]

---

[17] *Watching Slow Flowers*, p. 58.

Searching Energy + Stumping Mind

Using words to baffle the mind releases the brilliance
of the mind.

The language breaks. The mind is stopped.

When, barring understanding, words must instead
be grasped—

> thru Him marigold
> summertime
> summertime
> > bluefish
> > (pokeweed)
> > > WANTED
> > kept cups[18]

we hear the silence objectified.

---

[18] *Marginalia*, p. 94.

Disappearing Words

A word can be fused or rigidified into being
apparent, its nature frozen in space.

Taken apart, language is reamalgamated, releasing
the poor word from being so pinned down.

Moderating-the-deathly-state-of-being-signified
offers it up to a different kind of precision.

After all, the very unreality of compositional realism
points towards a stylistics that supports vanishing.

> *to be sky-full*
> once
>
> a rag of nods
> as the tide
>
> seeps in
>
> the camera
> of her
> (wanting numbers to fit)
>
> now and again
> an instant will finish[19]

[19] *Calliope*, p. 65.

Semiotics (words as symbols serving to convey meaning)

Words have a kind of television capacity. They captivate, distract and bring one to a zone of forgetting.

One feels the superficiality, the projection of an "I," the true or false identity and the meaninglessness, almost, of the very question of falseness.

Using words we fall into a similar stupor—replication where the machine of replication is forgotten or not considered.

Deadened by use we forget that words are signifiers, as we ourselves, outside the experience of "one taste," forget that this body is a sacred mandala for the victorious ones.

Gertrude Stein noticed. She spent her life as a nurse reinvigorating (resuscitating) flabby (traumatized) words.

Addressing questions of origin and responsibility, meaning grounds the mind in what it thinks it knows.

Refusing that releases the taste of what it cannot.

For poetic meaning accretes, not logically or deductively but through a process of settling.

Like a sensation that arises in sleep, of warmth and grace and sometimes intense feeling that adds up to, say, what a soul-catcher catches.

Poems of Origin

"Origin" (poetically) takes place every minute.

Existence, not locale, is the question.

To claim by language the source, this kind of accuracy, to own it with the word while the breathing of the poem (its contraction and widening) claims the paradox of its inexplicability.

> Earth overflows. That's what day breaks.
>
> Do you understand? (Many die confused.)
>
> Wandering through the *bardo*, the endless preserving of fat.
>
> I stare at the heavens just now cracked. Where in me is the vision of the great ones?[20]

We are the investor and the material word—its resonance of pain, the beauty of its failed dialogue . . .

The dialogue is beautiful *because* it fails, *because* of the impetus at its source.

The double-edge is *pronounced.*

[20] *DOHĀ*, p. 13.

Reading pain, the synovial fluid yoking word-breath-
life in perdurable somersault with word-death-life—
it's the joint venture of the cycle and the seeming
endlessness of the cycle.

Multi-dimensionality

surface beauty
meaning underlying the surface
an aha moment of true perception

     O'dear no the Prosepine
       to find
          the/
                (for one thing)
       reformation
       in
       hat

       curly mountains
          all
       up-to-up

       wants/
          to feel
        how
       much
       love
         how
       awakened intense
       ducks[21]

---

[21] unpublished

Here language and sexuality may be confused, the one propelling and originating the other.

Then a continuing sense of the power of sexuality and a deeper respect for its implications.

Finally the realization that desire—to communicate, to touch, to procreate and to exist—are all in fact one breath.

Breath IS creation. IS origin. We do not "contain" God; we *are* God and it is our will to exist and acquire that brings the world and its pain into being.

Acceptance of this responsibility opens the door to intimacy, perhaps our deepest form of grace (the grace of the world to speak intimately to us).

The world speaks its pain and its beauty—to see this in a material way—to simply stand and see.

Poetry is our cane.

Weight[22]

"Weight"—not of the poem (the *matter* of the poem) but the "hand" of the poet as she writes.

Like a pianist, a poet can bear down, but her bearing down is internal.

For language is an instrument that bears weight, dare one say, even more sensitively.

Not is good also. Not is a mechanism, like picking on a banjo, that to weight, by its nature, is impervious.

> *China bloodless boy*
>
> people of mast
> here are some
>
> if we are dumb
> if we are dumb
>
> so puffed and
> slobbering to themselves

*

---

[22] See David L. Sheidlower's review in Appendix I for further elucidation of this concept.

shouting it
down the mountain

lugging the beast
back to his people

*

over hills, over fields
the moon's condition
come to pass

come home stars
lay down your heads

nailed to the earth
across the pasture[23]

---

[23] *Calliope*, p. 14.

Meter

Take complexity + staccato.

Or leaving out an expected additional syllable.

> At length in kin beatitude

> At length in kin beatitude
> must as
> congenial amulet (person).
> Pardon me.
> Cutting the street
> the embankment
> (tourniquet)
> few thoughts reference[24]

A sustained jazzy meter can create a humorous continuum.

It helps one *depend*—hang upon or be contingently attached, even to the un-expressed.

---

[24] *Early Work*, p. 117.

Rhythm: the internal rhythm of a word and the overall river of words

Rhythm is the bedrock, the voice, the fundamental principle upon which a poem is built.

Rhythm *is* the "what" of what's being said because "how" is what's being said.

A continuous flow, for example, suggests that thoughts themselves are contiguous though not exactly *causing* one another.

Rhythm keeps the music clean. It *spells* the pulse of cyclical existence.

> *tiger tiger*
> from Yarlung Valley head
>
> arising from the flower
> from the bath
> of ancient wood
>
> Tara of the neck
> help me through
> this birth

draw the word
through its beauteous
hole[25]

---

[25] *Who, a* Licchavi, p. 27.

Linkage

Renga (Japanese) are linked poems of varying length launched by a *haiku*.

Often composed in a group setting, each poet jams off the previous poet's offering, grounding by links what otherwise might seem lame.[26]

The best links are invisible. They register, but on a first hit, not as a thought, but a flow.

Though *renga* are associated with *haiku*, the strategy, linkage, works just as well in other settings. (Note the current page and the one previous.)

---

[26] For an example, see: Gail Sher and Andrew Schelling, "Hundred-Stanza Renga," *Simply Haiku,* vol. 8, no. 2, Autumn 2010, simplyhaikujournal.com/autumn2010/rengags.htm.

Saturation

To saturate means to fill—to flood, glut, overload. To imbue or suffuse, to impregnate, permeate, steep.

Each word carries its absolute full load *so that* there is little distraction or waste of time (leakage).

The poet stuffs each word into a little canon.

It socks the reader.

Density

Puns, near-puns, verbal internal references,
grammatical sleights-of-hand, keep the weave of the
poem dense.

Take deliberate mis-use of grammar:

> Cleans the smile. Youngs girl.
> Come of its own (alone).[27]

The senseless plural echoes "cleans" and just barely
(gently) deflects the "young girl" pixels.

Confined contrasting feelings work similarly.

> A woman alone at a large open window
> gazes at the sky. The soft flesh of her arm
> folds around a basket. If she is dead, the
> colors may be alive.[28]

Sometimes a word careens out like a nightmare.

Or the gravitational pull of the poem's self-referents
may become so great that no light-of-import can
escape it for a reader.

---

[27] unpublished

[28] *Figures in Blue*, p. 1.

The poet cannot cheat.

If she loses track of her "coding system," her words are at risk of becoming black holes with little to inform them and keep them warm but their own sounds.

Simplicity

"Accurate" and "muscular" are two words that describe workable simplicity in a poem.

Its stark feet need to be stable. And flawless.

"Spare but right" holding its karma loosely.

As Hemingway taught, it requires a lot of control.

> *o buzzard in the sky*
> invoked the girl
> riding pillion[29]

---

[29] *old* dri's *lament,* p. 62.

"Equivalents" as Sub-logic or the Forgotten Vocabulary of a Word

Georgia O'Keefe used the term in this sense:

When she paints a flower she's not painting a flower but what she *feels* about the flower so if she chooses a line or a color to paint a geranium, for example, she may paint a green square which could be very exact.

Or how Swann in Proust's *Swann's Way* always did regard a phrase or musical motif as an idea, an actual conception veiled and impossible to know, but nonetheless distinct, unequal in value or significance.

In the same way words, as for a baby when it talks, behave with powerful though eclipsed intensity.

> A doll talks and if she's a tall doll, *in dependence on a listener*, her presence will not disperse far.

> Her body covers her life as if it were a cast.

> Mop-like braids fall to her waist. *If I were a Cyclops forging thunderbolts, I too would be being born* she posits.

A man binds his mind so that it doesn't
scatter. He tucks it between his breasts.
How have you left your mind before?
someone asks, speaking politely.[30]

---

[30] *though actually it is the same earth*, p. 38.

Restraint

Language is just language, "ghosted" as one critic of
my work said, "by the anxieties of actual experience,
ribboned by sexual shadings and innuendo, tense with
a pent energy resembling the un-had orgasm . . . so
that the hair of the language stiffens and all the tissue
is tight with implication unreleased."

Call it explosive reserve. Or "restraint," implying
holding back, curtailing, lopping, as in a harpsichord,
the gush, which by virtue of containment becomes
all the more eruptive.

Words are little volcanoes. The vortex, embedded
in the word, whirls around picking up particles via
energy, time, physical structure, psychology.

Lazy minds sleep. With convention snore.
Disruption wakes—to a fresh start, a new seeing, a
quick "Wait! Did you hear *that*?"

Masks: Catching the Surface with the Essence

"All profound things love the mask," said Nietzsche,
and for poetry masks write the dress-code.

> Not this couch hatch (hopes) like food . . . [31]

Masks loosen the mind and make a barrier around
the word so that its soul escapes to wander freely.

The gravity of time can easily make a word make
itself into a mask so that we can *tell* it's . . . what?
What is it precisely that we say, saying a word?

To satisfy a bias *for* the world, for descriptive writing
on no matter what descriptive level, or beyond mere
description to answer instead the riddle of what it is
to describe—

> the where-
> withal of birds
> flown/ from the
> evening and
> settled[32]

"This stanza works and I hardly know

---

[31] *Early Work*, p. 139.

[32] *Early Work*, p. 66.

why. It is vibrant, and multi-dimensional, and very glad and celestial," commented a reader.

Another: "I'm crazy about it. I can't even say why—I mean without "where-/withal" it wouldn't work, and how the rest of the words are seemingly so common, and yet one has created something extraordinarily perfect and beautiful. Like a haiku yes."

The "I hardly know why . . ."

Actually masks work by disburdening. The frontal lobes relax releasing a different kind of intelligence.

Relevance becomes implicit. It drifts around latching onto that or this or something that never happened.

Curiosity takes a stab. "Oh *I* know!" If there's an *I*, of course, we already know it doesn't, really, know anything of importance.

The journey, however, self-replicating and earnest, can be immensely revealing, transformational, and indeed "profound," to borrow Nietzsche's word.

The face beneath the mask may wear another mask but anyway will glow from the mere care of the person.

Titles

A title may name a poem but also spring out—be
energized by—the poem.

Or a title can *take place* in a poem unexpectedly, as if
stumbled over.

It can give information, create atmosphere,

    commodious dream to wherefore thou internal

        to beam/
            to is
      this
      sun[33]

"Here the stupendous length of the title is equal (in
some cosmic suchness value) to the brevity of the
poem. In fact the title partially *makes* the poem
through the sharp contrast of gloomy depths and
translucent light," one reader explained.

bliss and in her cabbage-petal fall the arch-meal's
bitterly, another title, is similar.

savannahs of the new world, another title, is similar.

---

[33] *Early Work*, p. 99.

Tricking you into the poem, a title may double cross

You avail yourself to language whose very nature
double crosses.

Colloquialisms, almost sloppy in the midst of
intense precision, surprise and slip you *between* the
cracks whose rough edges you might otherwise skirt
around.

These "lines you can trust" signify conclusions
ultimately not deducible.

      unravel Jacob

    prairies
       presses

        (juice
          of
         flowers)

     hovering
      like
    bread

           falling
          around

                         light

              lowering
                         steeples
              of
              thought[34]

A title may be inviting but not always inviting.

Sometimes they have the stereoscopic effect of
enlarging dimensions, lifting one out of what takes
place.

A title may point away but at the same time may
itself be the subject.

A title may point to a place unlocatable in the poem.

Setting up a poetic shiftiness.

The language proceeds with a duplicate motion that
consumes and sucks the wily words back in and you
end up, or start out, when the title does it too, in a
void.

---

[34] unpublished

The *Way* of the Living Word

The Body of the Word

The ordeal of a word is like trying to sleep with God.

The exchange is its offering.

We enter and awaken to our death and resurrection, if we're still enough, ripened enough.

The felt word, its intelligence, its thrall—inherent in its body is the *clear light* shining.

Take the word "spoon" with its energetic "p," its soothing "o's," the soft sound of its "n." The "s" of course risks getting tangled in the "p," but it's a good word, easy to use, respectable.

The sensual, obdurate "thing-ness" of its shape stands in its opacity purely for itself, leading to no other conclusion.

It doesn't ask to go further. It *refuses* to go further.

> Saw (too) to
> cling here
> chessmen[35]

is its own explication.

---

[35] *(As) on things which (headpiece) touches the Moslem*, unpaginated.

The Mind of the Word

Reaching for narrative, undermining narrative, taken alone, a word is a kind of narrative.

For time in a poem is discrete, and time in a word lets loose back to its own etymological pratfalls.

The vision may occur before imagination.

The event may sound prior to its happening.

The insouciance of a word . . .

The royalty of a word . . .

Eros lives in every word.

Through the eye of a word we see. (The *word* looks, from the vantage point of its mind.)

Disjuncture is its power, unhinged from meaning, bouncing off artifacts synonymous with an absence.

In a farrago of words, each word-moment is connected to all the others, the more seemingly unrelated, the stronger the psychic thread.

> A woman carries a jug dexterously embroidered on silk. The woman's skin shines like the interior pink of a river.
>
> The dimensions of the jug's magenta is implicit yet exacting.
>
> *Out* is not a direction but an aspect of conference around the jug's battered aggregates.
>
> Bringing yellow *out*, where *out* is a structure of color *and* light, intensifies *out*, as if its DNA changes.[36]

---

[36] *though actually it is the same earth*, p. 23.

A word reveals a healthy lust for the innards of its survival.

One whishes you up into a vacuum where there is no placement, no resolution, nothing that can be returned to.

Its performance leaves no trace (though there is something so familiar).

Held there in your wanting, you reach, you stretch and the stretching opens and deepens what you feel so that *almost* becomes an invitation and at the same time an entrance to what finally gives way to another name.

The Transmission of a Word

The Path of each word decouples its identity.

Different contexts feature different *parts*.

Also different *paths*. The Path of a word has trails
that carry the word even into the midst of the bodies
of other words.

Thus we have the word, its figuration in a different
word, and the meditation in our mind of the
marriage of the two thereafter.

Marriage, a sacrament, includes an oath made with
words.

For God and Word are the same, plucked from the
same stream.

However remote, something of that consecration
lingers—as we are using words, contemplating
words—as Ted Hughes' phrase "achieved human
voice" ratifies.

His heightened relationship with words elevates this
awareness, but for all who care, all who attend, the
transmission is there along with the respect of the
word.

Late Work

Late work (the poetry I began writing in 2014)
addresses a different part of the brain than my earlier
work.

The element of space directs itself no longer to
wisdom mind but to lesser-exalted areas of the self,
not necessarily pre-verbal.

That human beings are primarily relational takes on
new significance.

Formerly silence was *in* the word and *was* the word
(introverted). Now it is also referential (extroverted).

> New Year's Eve
> listen—
> snow is falling[37]

Sensation becomes memory.

What erupts may be from the reptilian brain but may
also stem from more highly evolved areas.

Meaning extends beyond the word into clusters of

---

[37] *Pale Sky*, p. 10.

words, sentences and remainders after the sentences
have passed.

> The mind of the woman is warm, her
> sweaters and chickens and all the places on
> the boat . . .

> "Hello," Unn offers.

> "What?" shouts the woman.[38]

Meaning finally is useful. Before, it not only was not
useful, it obstructed what was useful.

Before there was the boat. Now there's the other
shore.

The *device*—thinking you know what it means—
becomes authenticated by the text—you *do* know
what it means.

> She wondered if the fact that things ceased
> to exist in her meant that they ceased to
> exist.

> Does time cease to exist or does it flow
> parallel to what looks like one's existence?

---

[38] *Sunny Day, Spring*, p. 3.

What is one's existence? What is the
relation between time and one's existence?[39]

It means what it means to you, but meaning is
intended whereas in the earlier work, the flow *toward*
meaning was simply bait.

---

[39] *Ezekiel*, p. 78.

Appendix I

ANDREW SCHELLING
Gail Sher: Poetry 1981-2006
A review essay

I first met Gail Sher in the early nineteen-eighties when we were both living in Berkeley. I'd already read her earliest published poetry and heard friends speak about her practice of both Buddhism and writing. In a modest way she was a legend among local poets & Zen students. When I actually met her, she was finishing up a book of bread recipes, an activity less surprising in those days than it might seem now.

The story about Gail's poetry was that she'd begun to write her tough, multi-layered, flint-like poems, often in series, while a student at Zen Center's Tassajara Mountain retreat. She had continued to write as a daily discipline after returning to the East Bay where she dwelt on the far fringes of the energetic language poetry crowd. The earliest events she and I appeared at together were conversations about poetry and Buddhist practice—once in San Francisco, once at Green Gulch Zen Center near Muir Beach. To my imagination though, she remained a figure of Tassajara.

Tassajara lies in one of those cañados that in summer visiting season crackles with tough, aromatic brush—as well as manzanita & poison oak—deep in the mountains inland from Monterey. The site, along a boulder strewn creek, was first known to native peoples for its healing hot springs. You can only readily get there during the dry season, & only with a serviceable car, standard transmission, to take you seven miles uphill, then seven precipitous miles down a harrowing dirt road. The road twists along a valley wall held in place by the roots of dwarf oaks. When I'd visit in the seventies and eighties, I went in my big, square '64 Pontiac, which burnt through its brakes the first time down. From then on the car stayed at China Camp, a hilltop site with primitive facilities. Seven miles down to Tassajara by foot— bathe in the creek, drink tea generously provided by the Zen Students, buy a loaf of Tassajara's renowned bread, sit zazen in the zendo—then trudge seven miles back to the clatter of crickets. On one of those

trips I heard of a poet who had taken to a daily
practice of writing, and did it as a solitary discipline.
So different from the gregarious poets I knew in the
Bay Area!

When I found Gail's books, I imagined her having
stepped from a Japanese Noh play. Her poems,
sharpened by rigorous Buddhist discipline—& not to
everybody's taste—grabbed me instantly. They were
tough, refreshingly hard-edged, full of the natural
world—constructed of bits and pieces of mineral,
insect, bark, summer grass. They could cry out from
the page in several languages at once, with English
functioning (I thought) like a piece of steel to strike
the spark. They felt classical. Despite their wild
turns of phrasing, fox barks & cricket clicks, under
the surface they showed a sensibility that was refined,
educated, attentive to natural detail, & enamored of
the chipped, the asymmetric, the rustic. They put
me in mind of the writers of Japan's Heian court, the
best of whom were women. I still hear echoes of
Murasaki Shikibu or Ono no Komachi when I open
Gail's books.

My ear had been tuned to Modernist rhythms

& syntax by Pound's *Cantos* and his haunting
translation of Noh plays. I'd been schooled in the
compressed poems of Lorine Niedecker and the
Objectivists, had started to collect the crisp haiku-
inflected translations of American Indian poems
done by Frances Densmore, and gotten first-hand
know-how of Asian poetry through the mustard-
crackling syllables of Sanskrit. When I found Gail's
poems, they became instant companions. I knew she
was up to something special. *(As) on things which
(headpiece) touches the Moslem* was probably the
book that first showed me how my own generation's
often extreme experiments with language—cracking
words apart & recombining syllables or sentences
in ways that carried ear & mind to completely new
realms—could be more than politically radical. They
could be ecologically radical, spiritually radical.

I remember many poems by Philip Whalen & Diane
di Prima also written at Tassajara, and maybe some
by Norman Fischer or Pat Reed. Once on the twisty,
uphill walk back to China Camp through burnt-over
oaks—frightening wildfire had raced through in '77
or '78—ghost faces leapt out where the firefighter's

axes had slashed through scorched trunks and exposed bright inner wood. I composed a lengthy poem (thankfully lost long ago) to capture the California landscape with its Zen center, lizards, and rattlesnakes. Of all the writing Tassajara's inspired, though, Gail Sher's must be the most fully generated out of that canyon, its geothermal forces, its healing hot springs.

Gail has worked with, & been instrumental in naturalizing to our North American continent, several Asian poetic traditions. This is something only a Left Coast or Pacific Rim poet could do with ease, and a direct if invisible lineage runs through her from the Far East. She has worked haiku and its linked-verse cousin renku. She has written an autobiographical account of her Buddhist training in haibun form. More recently, familiarity with yoga practice has drawn her to India's musical tradition, and the outcome of this was the serial poem RAGA. In conversation with Tibetan Buddhism, she also wrote *DOHĀ* , a book modeled on Tibetan songs of devotion and instruction.

Every plant, wild animal, watershed, well-crafted

building, every poem or human being, holds a
quality that is the root of its life and spirit. This
quality is quite sharp, objective, wise. It is also
creative and fluid so cannot be caught or described.
Matsuo Basho found this spirit to animate haiku,
lyric poems, the tea ceremony, archery. It runs
through all of Gail Sher's poetry—loose, alive,
relaxed, content with imperfection, winding around
an inward mystery. Her writing reveals the finely
edged relationship between ourselves and our
surroundings. When I go to her poetry I do it the
way I hike into the mountains or up a gorge, or for
that matter step into a temple or meditation hall. I
find things fully alive there. Not opinions, ideas,
notions—just the wild spirit of living things.

What is the natural habitat of North American
poetry if not the great ecosystem of the Small Press?
An ecosystem comprised of energy pathways,
migration corridors, nutrient exchanges. It is alive
with life & death chases, sweeping unpredictable
weather patterns, and acts of breath-taking
generosity. Gail's poems saw light here: Rosmarie &
Keith Waldrop's Burning Deck Press, Matt & Sarah

Correy's Rodent Press, Joey Simas's Moving Letters. But the world of publishing got rougher in the 1990's (absorption of corporate publishing houses into media empires, overthrow of distributors who handle small presses). One response has been for poets to consolidate their resources. Gail's poetry has moved to a new home, Night Crane Press.

Small and micro presses serving the San Francisco Bay Area have taken totem animals for a long time. White Rabbit, Grey Fox, Coyote Books. Turtle Island fits in too. Now Night Crane, with its whiff of transient life, is collecting Gail Sher's poetry into an online edition. This is a wonderful gathering. Much in these books will be rough going, though, even for seasoned readers. Tibetan words, Sanskrit, Hebrew, Japanese. Syllables cobbled into seed-like stanzas that don't easily crack. Of course poetry has always been hard to crack. "Don't follow in the steps of the old masters," said one old master, "seek what they sought." What a hard lesson.

Fourth of July Valley
May 31, 2006

DAVID L. SHEIDLOWER

Miming the Phrase
Review of *(As) on things which (headpiece) touches
the Moslem* by Gail Sher (San Francisco: Square Zero
Editions, 1982).

Gail Sher places an incredible weight <u>in</u> each phrase
of this book. They <u>are</u> phrases mostly, the discreet
& seemingly incomplete units which make up this
short book. I find the weight in the phrases, not
on them; they are not burdened, rather each has
its own volume & density, can attract the phrases
around them or be inert and integral. Take the
phrase: "Tubers & iron/even to prepare/this." From
their natural state, both the vegetable & the mineral
are prepared by heat, in that sense they're even (or
equal). Very dense consistencies also. Then the
"this" which, locating only itself (i.e. not subordinate
as in "this thing here") pulls down on the three words
above it & the question is not "even to prepare this
what?," but can the middle phrase double itself?
Rather than one incomplete phrase, there are two
phrases here, with "even" meaning "as well" and
"equal" simultaneously.

A line by itself reads: "Mime is first"; and yes the words are, at first reading, gestures of phrases. Like a mime (on a still, empty stage) pretending to be thrown forward by the short stop of a bus he's not riding on, these phrases imitate the motion of phrases in a context, but are surrounded by white space & make their own sense: "Dawns or/parson."

The next line is "Or go god," That's a real choice in this poem which invites speculation on whether or not religious characters (specific & general): "monk", "god", "nun", "Christ", "the Moslem"), religious actions (vowing, chanting, renunciating, gracing) & religious imagery ("the/shepherd", "The wooly flesh") can maintain their religious meanings in such undevotional as well as non-moralistic phrases. And of course they can if you let them.

The poem is not didactic, offers choices. Hence, the only pronunciation is a handful of parentheses at the beginning which sets the mood for the optional: "Saw (too) to/cling here"; take or leave either "to" or "too" or both. Some phrases end with "this" or begin with "As," attracting surrounding phrases (but there is no syllogistic sense which definitely connects any

two phrases and hence the connections are optional).
The poem offers the choice between action and
being: "A rung or yelling," "The grit or/hear"; but
wonderfully & conscientiously blurs the distinction
between the two "As hover from the/elbows is
something/growing." And so the distinctions
between mime and the actual are blurred.

Berkeley, 1982

GAIL SHER

Letter to the Editor of *The San Francisco Review of
Books* (June 1979) [40]

Dear Mr. Nowicki,

Last night I read the following in a story called "The
thrower-away" by Heinrich Boll:

> ...I am making an intensive study of a
> young man from my neighborhood who
> earned his living as a book reviewer but at
> times was unable to practice his profession
> because he found it impossible to undo the
> twisted wire tied around the parcel, and
> even when he did find himself equal to
> this physical exertion, he was incapable of
> penetrating the massive layer of gummed
> paper with which the corrugated paper is
> stuck together. The man appears deeply
> disturbed and has now gone over to
> reviewing the books unread and placing the
> parcels on his bookshelves without

---

[40] My first published writing defends another writer, Barabara
Einzig, but it somehow describes the kind of writing I end up
doing myself thirty years later in my "late work."

> unwrapping them. I leave it to the reader's
> imagination to depict for himself the effect
> of such a case on our intellectual life.

and wondered if this could be the problem in the style of the reviewer of "Some Problems of Style" in Barbara Einzig's *Disappearing Work* and if so, should we be glad or sorry that so much potential is being "thrown away" as it were. Perhaps something could be done to help the matter along, for example the reviewer might appreciate receiving an unwrapped copy of the above mentioned book. I myself would be happy to provide him with one. He could then have the pleasure of easily reading it and I'm sure upon so doing he will notice immediately that though indeed novel it is not a novel at all, though full of precision it has no chronology (the first section is later than the second), it has no "protagonist" and is not "just another" anything but an entirely unique (not story) but brilliantly executed expose of the unconscious male or female.

Apologies are in order. They would do wonders for the fast failing reputation of SFRB not to mention the alleviating effect they might have, if it's not too late, on our intellectual life.[41]

San Francisco
May 8, 1979

---

[41] The editor replied, "Whether or not Einzig's book is categorized as a novel, my opinion remains that it is flat and too low-key to arouse the reader's interest. . . ."

Appendix II

A Personal Chronology of External Life Circumstances

1942: Born in St. Louis, Missouri's Jewish Hospital.

1947-53: Elementary school in University City, a suburb of St. Louis.

1954-57: Hanley Junior High School in University City.

1958-60: University City Senior High School (avid reader, diary writer and aspiring pianist studying with Harold Zabrach).

1960-61: University of Florida, Gainesville (study piano, music history, composition, theory).

1961-62: Hebrew University, Jerusalem (study Hebrew, Torah and piano at the Jerusalem Academy of Music).

1962-64: BA in English at Northwestern University. Receive Ford Foundation Fellowship to study linguistics at the University of Texas at Austin.

1964: Choose instead to study Middle English at the University of California, Berkeley; meet Arthur Weiner, fellow graduate student in English and reader for the poet Thom Gunn.

1965: Arthur and I marry.

1966: Receive a secondary teaching credential from U.C. Berkeley.

1966-68: Enjoy teaching high school English at Ygnacio Valley High and Pleasant Hill High; win "Teacher of the Year" Award from three education faculties (Stanford, Berkeley, San Francisco State). Have a harpsichord built and begin studying harpsichord with a very gifted teacher, Jean Nandi, a student of Gustav Leonhardt.[42]

November 1968: Arthur and I separate; I begin sitting zazen at the Berkeley Zendo (part of the San Francisco Zen Center).

Summer 1969: Attend Summer Practice Period at Tassajara Zen Mountain Center with Suzuki-roshi.

---

[42] For more on Jean Nandii's unconventional, inspiring life, see *Unconventional Wisdom: A Memoir* by Jean Nandi, downloadable at www.elverhoj.org/archives/nandi.html.

Fall 1969: Move into the Berkeley Zendo; and, encouraged by Jean Nandi, begin a second BA, in music, at UC Berkeley.

1971: Move to San Francisco Zen Center and Tassajara Zen Mountain Center in order to practice Zen full-time; ordained a lay disciple of Suzuki-roshi.

1980: Leave Zen Center after eleven years, realizing that my practice needs to be *writing*.[43] I had already abandoned the formal practice of music, consciously dedicating my musical ability to writing, selling my harpsichord and donating the proceeds to purchase a great temple bell, crafted in Japan, for Zen Center.

1980: I move to an apartment on Haight Street and begin writing daily, publishing poems in small literary journals. Become friends with Beau

---

[43] *Moon of the Swaying Buds* describes how I came to this decision. Through Zen I discover "Yes Practice": only doing those things I can say Yes to with my whole body and mind. By then, however, "I am through with Zen Center. I need to define my own regime. Zen Center has had it with me anyway. I am told privately that unless my attitude changes, I will not be accepted for Fall Practice Period. Indeed, my attitude has changed but not in the direction that would pique my interest in Fall Practice Period" (*Moon of the Swaying Buds,* 2001, p.392).

Beausoleil, Leslie Scalapino and Merry Benezra.

1982: Move to Etna St. in Berkeley; work as personal assistant for Billy & Alice Shapiro; continue writing daily and begin publishing books of poetry with small, independent presses.

1982-1993: Yoga-based meditation practice with Self Realization Fellowship. I am attracted to this heart-based practice, which complements the mind-based Zen I knew; I especially appreciate that this community, founded by Paramahansa Yogananda in the 1920s, is led by women.

1985-1990 Complete MA in Clinical Psychology at John F. Kennedy University; meet Brendan Collins, former Benedictine monk, photographer, teacher and psychologist.

1990: Brendan and I marry; I begin private practice as psychotherapist; continue publishing with small presses.

1995: Meet Adzom Paylo Rinpoche, meditation master in the Nyingma tradition of Tibetan Buddhism, and begin a concentrated study of

Tibetan Buddhism; complete the *Longchen Nyingthig Ngondro* under his direction and guidance. This form of Buddhism brings together the heart *and* mind practice I have long sought.

1997-continuing: After the closing of so many small independent presses, Brendan and I establish Night Crane Press; I continue writing early every morning, working as a psychotherapist, practicing Tibetan Buddhism, and enjoying living with Brendan.

An Internal History of My Relationship with Language

"The literary persona who enacts the
poet's struggle can be glimpsed, always, in
one early work that Ted Hughes calls the
'first,' which contains, in a single image,
'a package of precisely folded, multiple
meanings.' The origin of this image is a
trauma, usually hidden from the writer's
consciousness, that partakes in a wholly
personal way of some destructive aspect of
cultural life." [44]

The dates are vague. We live on an army base in
North Carolina where my father, Charles Sher, is
stationed.

While he is overseas, I live with my mother, her
three volatile sisters, her absent father, nervous-
breakdown-prone mother, and a slightly older, noisy
and aggressive male cousin. In this household—I am
two—I begin stuttering and am diagnosed with

---

[44] Diane Middlebrook, *Her Husband: Ted Hughes and Sylvia
Plath—A Marriage* (New York: Penguin, 2003), p. 245.

a "nervous breakdown." The symptoms—stuttering, hypervigilance and nonadaptability to change— are consistent with recent research on pre-school children in traumatic, disruptive, unpredictable environments.

I am removed to the apartment of my paternal grandmother who says to my mother, "You can live here but I'm not paying for her milk."

With his impressive purple heart my war veteran father returns. "Honey, that's your father." "No it's not. *This* is my father," I say, pointing to his photograph. I believe I am four.

A primary memory is sitting on an outside step striving toward collecting all my words and feeling extremely frustrated that I do not know how to write.

My hysterical mother and war-traumatized father fight constantly (about money and sexual transgressions on both parts).

I act out in elementary school. Feel very very ugly. Take refuge in reading the interesting books provided by my mother.

I rock in bed, at my desk in school, in my rocking chair when I am reading.

Begin to adjust socially in 9th grade, become a cheerleader and am liked by boys, but I cannot think analytically and only do average in my classes, which feels not only humiliating but somehow wrong (incorrect).

In 10th grade an English teacher compliments what she calls a "parallel structure" that I use inadvertently. On the spot I decide to become a writer but am discouraged by my father who says, "Oh everyone wants to be *that.*"

Thinking and writing analytically continue to be problems all the way through graduate school, though at Northwestern I devised a way to pass written exams, receive my B.A. and a Ford Foundation Fellowship to study linguistics.

Meanwhile in high school, in an outside study, I test at the 99th percentile in math and language, and have been in a longitudinal study for gifted children ever since. (I am now 73.)

Oddly (to me) I feel I "belong" in the gifted group yet consistently my drifting mind and grades do not back that up

Eventually I have the following thought: "I CAN'T see white like everyone else, but the black I see is not nothing. It is rich and full of music." I begin to feature it in my stabs at writing (having still the sense that I do not know what I'm doing, but liking the result).

The thought that it is something is a turning point.

Based on recent research on the neurological effect of trauma, my frontal lobes probably were dysfunctional, but my implicit memories and awareness were not dysfunctional. Since this is all I have, I lavish my attention on THAT.

I discover that I am hyper-aware of aspects about language that most people ignore.

With years of disciplined Buddhist practice behind me, I force myself to write from the *right* side of my brain and discover a whole new relationship with words.

In retrospect I feel that were it not for the trauma—whose effect was at the forefront through my thirties, into my forties and to some extent is *still* present—I would not have seen, certainly not so clearly, the contents of the space brightened by a shut-down left frontal cortex.

I feel grateful for the passion that insisted on a way, and eventually found a way, and made it *my* WAY.

Bibliography

Poetry Books by Gail Sher organized by phase:

1. RADICAL LANGUAGE EXPERIMENTS, 1982-1997

From another point of view the woman seems to be resting. San Francisco: Trike, 1982.

(As) on things which (headpiece) touches the Moslem. San Francisco: Square Zero, 1982.

Rouge to beak having me. Paris: Moving Letters Press, 1983.

Broke Aide. Providence: Burning Deck, 1985.

Cops. Berkeley: Little Dinosaur, 1988.

KUKLOS. Providence: Paradigm Press, 1995.

la. Boulder: Rodent Press, 1996.

Marginalia. Chicago: Rodent Press, 1997.

Early Work. Emeryville, CA: Night Crane Press, 2016.

2. ASIAN-INFLUENCED WORK, 1996-2008

Five Haiku Narratives Emeryville, CA: Night Crane Press. 2015.[45]

Moon of the Swaying Buds. Emeryville, CA: Night Crane Press, 2001.

Look at That Dog All Dressed Out in Plum Blossoms. Emeryville, CA: Night Crane Press, 2002.

RAGA. Emeryville, CA: Night Crane Press, 2004.

redwing daylong daylong. Emeryville, CA: Night Crane Press, 2004.

Once There Was Grass. Emeryville, CA: Night Crane Press, 2004.

DOHĀ. Emeryville, CA: Night Crane Press, 2005.

Watching Slow Flowers. Emeryville, CA: Night Crane Press, 2006.

---

[45] Contains the following out-of-print chapbooks written between 1996-2002: *Like a Crane at Night* (1996); *One Bug ... One Mouth ... Snap!* (1997); *Saffron Wings* (1998); *Fifty Jigsawed Bones* (1999); *Lines: The Life of a Laysan Albatross* (2002).

The Haiku Masters: Four Poetic Diaries. Emeryville, CA: Night Crane Press, 2008.

3. THE WISDOM-MIND COLLECTION, 2008-2013

though actually it is the same earth. Emeryville, CA: Night Crane Press, 2008.

The Tethering of Mind to Its Five Permanent Qualities. Emeryville, CA: Night Crane Press, 2009.

Mother's Warm Breath. Emeryville, CA: Night Crane Press, 2010.

White Bird. Emeryville, CA: Night Crane Press, 2010.

The Bardo Books. Emeryville, CA: Night Crane Press, 2011.

Figures in Blue. Emeryville, CA: Night Crane Press, 2012.

The Twelve Nidānas. Emeryville, CA: Night Crane Press, 2012.

Mingling the Threefold Sky. Emeryville, CA: Night Crane Press, 2013.

4. LATE WORK, 2014-PRESENT

Sunny Day, Spring. Emeryville, CA: Night Crane Press, 2014.

Ezekiel. Emeryville, CA: Night Crane Press, 2015.

Pale Sky. Emeryville, CA: Night Crane Press, 2015.

Elm (in press).

Publications by Gail Sher by date, 1981-2016

All of Gail Sher's poetry in books and in journals is online at: gailsher.com and at: library.buffalo.edu/collections/gail-sher.

Print copies of her books and the journals in which she has appeared are in the Poetry Collection of the University at Buffalo (SUNY).

Books published by Night Crane Press remain in print and can be ordered from any bookseller, including online sellers.

PROSE BOOKS (PRINT)

Reading Gail Sher. Emeryville, CA: Night Crane Press, 2016.

Poetry, Zen and the Linguistic Unconscious. Emeryville, CA: Night Crane Press, 2016.

Writing the Fire: Yoga and the Art of Making Your Words Come Alive. New York: Random House/Bell Tower, 2006.

The Intuitive Writer: Listening to Your Own Voice. New York: Penguin, 2002.

One Continuous Mistake: Four Noble Truths for Writers. New York: Penguin, 1999.

From a Baker's Kitchen: Techniques and Recipes for Quality Baking in the Home Kitchen. Twentieth Anniversary Edition. New York: Marlow & Co., 2004.

From a Baker's Kitchen: Techniques and Recipes for Professional Quality Baking in the Home Kitchen. Berkeley: Aris Books, 1984.

POETRY BOOKS (PRINT)

Early Work. Emeryville, CA: Night Crane Press, 2016.

Pale Sky. Emeryville, CA: Night Crane Press. 2015.

Five Haiku Narratives. Emeryville, CA: Night Crane Press. 2015.

Ezekiel. Emeryville, CA: Night Crane Press, 2015.

Sunny Day, Spring. Emeryville, CA: Night Crane Press, 2014.

Mingling the Threefold Sky. Emeryville, CA: Night Crane Press, 2013.

The Twelve Nidānas. Emeryville, CA: Night Crane Press, 2012.

Figures in Blue. Emeryville, CA: Night Crane Press, 2012.

The Bardo Books. Emeryville, CA: Night Crane Press, 2011.

White Bird. Emeryville, CA: Night Crane Press, 2010.

Mother's Warm Breath. Emeryville, CA: Night Crane Press, 2010.

The Tethering of Mind to Its Five Permanent Qualities.
Emeryville, CA: Night Crane Press, 2009.

though actually it is the same earth. Emeryville, CA:
Night Crane Press, 2008.

The Haiku Masters: Four Poetic Diaries. Emeryville,
CA: Night Crane Press, 2008.

Who, a Licchavi. Emeryville, CA: Night Crane Press,
2007.

Calliope. Emeryville, CA: Night Crane Press, 2007.

old dri's *lament.* Emeryville, CA: Night Crane Press,
2007.

The Copper Pheasant Ceases Its Call. Emeryville, CA:
Night Crane Press, 2007.

East Wind Melts the Ice. Emeryville, CA: Night Crane
Press, 2007.

Watching Slow Flowers. Emeryville, CA: Night Crane
Press, 2006.

DOHĀ. Emeryville, CA: Night Crane Press, 2005.

RAGA. Emeryville, CA: Night Crane Press, 2004.

Once There Was Grass. Emeryville, CA: Night Crane Press, 2004.

redwing daylong daylong. Emeryville, CA: Night Crane Press, 2004.

Birds of Celtic Twilight: A Novel in Verse. Emeryville, CA: Night Crane Press, 2004.

Look at That Dog All Dressed Out in Plum Blossoms. Emeryville, CA: Night Crane Press, 2002.

Lines: The Life of a Laysan Albatross. Emeryville, CA: Night Crane Press, 2002 [reprinted in *Five Haiku Narratives*].

Moon of the Swaying Buds. San Francisco: Edgework, 2002.

Moon of the Swaying Buds (Limited Edition). Emeryville, CA: Night Crane Press, 2001.

Fifty Jigsawed Bones: A Sea Turtle's Life. Emeryville, CA: Night Crane Press, 2001 [reprinted in *Five Haiku Narratives*].

Saffron Wings. Berkeley: Night Crane Press, 1998 [reprinted in *Five Haiku Narratives*]. .

One bug . . . one mouth . . . snap! A Year in the Life of a Turtle. Berkeley: Night Crane Press, 1997 [reprinted in *Five Haiku Narrative*].

Marginalia. Chicago: Rodent Press, 1997.

la. Boulder: Rodent Press, 1996.

Like a Crane at Night. Berkeley: Night Crane Press, 1996 [reprinted in *Five Haiku Narratives*].

KUKLOS. Providence: Paradigm Press, 1995.

Cops. Berkeley: Little Dinosaur, 1988.

Broke Aide. Providence: Burning Deck, 1985.

Rouge to beak having me. Paris: Moving Letters Press, 1983.

(As) on things which (headpiece) touches the Moslem. San Francisco: Square Zero, 1982.

From another point of view the woman seems to be resting. San Francisco: Trike, 1982.

PERIODICALS & ANTHOLOGIES

"Excerpt from *Blue*." *Al-Mutanabbi Street Starts Here*. Eds. Beau Beausoleil & Deema K. Shehabi. Oakland, CA: PM Press, 2012. 71. Print.

"Hundred-Stanza Renga" [with Andrew Schelling], *Simply Haiku*, 8.2, Autumn 2010, simplyhaikujournal.com/autumn2010/rengags.htm.

"can't touch you" [with David Rice]. *The Tanka Journal* 14. Tokyo: Nihon Kajin Club [Japan Tanka Poets' Club], 1999. 10. Print.

"Lovers" [nine poems]. *Generator* 8.1: *A Magazine of International Experimental Visual and Language Material*. Cleveland, OH: Generator Press, 1998. n.p. Print.

"Autumn" [includes Japanese translation]. *Ashiya International Haiku Festa 1998*. [Award]. Ashiya, Hyogo, Japan: 1998. 36. Print.

"Against the longed-for clouds" [with David Rice]. *Tanka Splendor 1997*. [Award]. Gualala, CA: AHA Books, 1997. n.p. Print.

"Fallout." [Honorable Mention]. *Hiroshima Haiku and Tanka Competition*, 1997. n.p. Print.

"Silent snow." *One Breath: Haiku Society of America 1995 Members' Anthology*. New York: Haiku Society of America, 1996. 14. Print,

"Basho." *Black Bough* 8. Flemington, NJ: 1996. 5. Print.

"The Paintings of Social Concern." *Juxta* 4. Charlottesville, VA: 1996. n.p. Print.

"Wipers steady," "Home at last," "Night Falls" [corrected version]. *Frogpond* 19.1. New York: Haiku Society of America, 1996. 8, 20, 52. Print.

"Innocent Diversions" *Chain* 3. *Special Topic: Hybrid Genres/Mixed Media*. Buffalo: 1996. 183-188. Print.

"Night falls," *Woodnotes* 28. [Associate Editor: Gail Sher]. Foster City, CA, Spring 1996. 9. Print.

"The boy dozes," "Winter sun." *Woodnotes* 29 [Associate Editor: Gail Sher]. Foster City, CA, Summer, 1996. 10, 22. Print.

"George Tooker: Marginalia" [excerpt]. *Big Allis 7*.

Brooklyn: 1996. 30-33. Print.

"Autumn leaves." *Ant 3: A Periodical of Autochthonous Poetry & Other Conundrums.* Oakland, CA, Summer 1996. n.p. Print.

"Resurrection," "The Seven Sacraments." *Raddle Moon* 15. Vancouver, BC, Canada, 1996. 113-118. Print.

"Noisy city." *Raw NerVZ* 2.4. Aylmer, QC, Canada: Proof Press, Winter 1995-96. 29. Print.

"Winds blow briskly this evening." *Five Lines Down: A Tanka Journal.* Redwood City, CA: Winter 1995. 12. Print.

"Even in his company," "The wind blows stronger." *Woodnotes,* 25. San Francisco: Haiku Poets of Northern California, Summer 1995. 8, 13. Print.

"Cross-legged I sit." *Ant* 2. Oakland, CA: Summer 1995. n.p. Print.

"Home at last" [includes Japanese translation]. *Basho Festival Dedicatory Anthology.* [Award]. Ueno City, Mie Prefecture, Japan: Master Basho Museum, 1995. n.p. Print.

"Night falls." *Woodnotes* 26. San Francisco: Haiku Poets of Northern California, Autumn 1995. 24. Print.

"Snow buries," " A train whistle blows," "Tassajara Summer 1969." *Woodnotes* 27. San Francisco: Haiku Poets of Northern California, Winter 1995. 17, 31, 41. Print.

"Folding its wings." *Modern Haiku,* 26.1. Madison, WI: 1995. 10. Print.

"Sudden squall," "Misty rain." *Frogpond* 18.3. New York, NY: Haiku Society of America, Autumn 1995. 22, 37. Print.

"Night Falls." *Frogpond* 18.4. New York, NY: Haiku Society of America, Winter 1995. 21. Print.

"Silent snow." *Woodnotes* 23. San Francisco: Haiku Poets of Northern California, Winter 1994. 5. Print.

"la" [excerpt]. *Big Allis* 5. New York, 1992. 34-41. Print.

"Ex voto" [excerpt from *Broke Aide* (1985) translated into French by Pierre Alferi & Joseph Simas]. *49+1:*

Nouveaux Poètes Américains. Eds. Emmanuel Hocquard & Claude Royet-Journoud. Royaumont (France): 1991. 222-223. Print.

"Osiris co rider" [from "Kuklos"]. *Gallery Works* 8. Aptos, CA: 1991. n.p. Print.

"Tamarind Esau" [from "Kuklos"]. *Big Allis* 1. New York: 1989. Print.

"W/" *Abacus* 35. Elmwood, CT: Potes & Poets Press: 1988. n.p. Print.

"The Fasting Spirit." [review essay on anorexia nervosa, with excerpts from "Moon of the Swaying Buds"]. *The San Francisco Jung Institute Library Journal,* 8:2. San Francisco: 1988. 61-80. Print.

Starving passion: A Tribute to Anorexia. Thesis (M.A.), John F. Kennedy University, 1988, listed in: catalog.jfku.edu; print copy in the Gail Sher Collection, Poetry Collection, University at Buffalo (SUNY).

"Cops" [excerpt read by Gail Sher at UCSD November 24, 1987]. *Archive Newsletter: The Archive of New Poetry.* San Diego: University of California,

1987. 12-14. Print.

"Cops" [excerpt]. *Writing* 18. Vancouver BC, Canada: 1987. Print.

Ten poems. *Gallery Works* 7. Norwalk, CT: 1987. n.p. Print.

"For Bart II." *Karamu,* 10:2. Charleston, IL: Eastern Illinois Univeristy, 1987. 14-19. Print.

"The Lanyard." *Notus: New Writing,* 1:1. Ann Arbor: 1986. 13-21. Print.

"For Bart." *Tramen,* 4. San Francisco: 1985. n.p. Print.

"Which Collateral Bends the Sea," "Deft and Resilient." *Gallery Works* 6. Bronx, NY: 1984. n.p. Print.

Poems. *Credences: A Journal of Twentieth Century Poetry and Poetics,* New Series 3:1. Buffalo: State University of New York, 1984. 84-88. Print.

"From Another Point of View the Woman Seems To Be Resting." *Credences: A Journal of Twentieth Century Poetry and Poetics,* New Series 2:1, Buffalo: State University of New York, 1982. 9-11. Print.

"Suppose deeply offers up." *Hambone* 2. Santa Cruz, CA, 1982. 18-22. Print.

"River the Office My Own," "Lord and Give the Necklace Back." *Gallery Works* 5. Bronx, NY: 1981. n.p. Print.

Poems. *Gnome Baker* 7 & 8 (1981): n.p. [10 pages]. Print.

Nine Pieces. *Credences: A Journal of Twentieth Century Poetry and Poetics,* New Series 1:1, Buffalo: State University of New York, 1981. 16-20. Print.

Reading Gail Sher
is set in Minion, a typeface designed by
Robert Slimbach in the spirit of the humanist
typefaces of fifteenth-century Venice; it was
released by Adobe Systems in 1990.
Cover design: Bryan Kring

www.ingramcontent.com/pod-product-compliance
Lightning Source LLC
Chambersburg PA
CBHW071009040426
42443CB00007B/732